C000142405

Exploring Cornwall
with your car

Tor Mark Press · Penryn

Other books in this series

Antiquities of the Cornish Countryside
Birds of Cornwall
China clay
Cornish Folklore
Cornish Legends
Cornish Mining – Underground
Cornish Mining – at the Surface
Cornish Recipes
Cornwall's Early Lifeboats
Cornwall's Engine Houses
Cornwall's Railways
Historic Houses, Castles and Gardens
Introducing Cornwall
Pebbles on Cornish Beaches
Seashells on Cornish Beaches
Shipwrecks – St Ives to Bude
Shipwrecks Around Land's End
Shipwrecks Around the Lizard
The Story of Cornwall
The Story of Cornwall's Churches
The Story of the Cornish Language
The Story of St Ives
Surfing South-West
Tales of the Cornish Fishermen
Tales of the Cornish Miners
Tales of the Cornish Smugglers
Tales of the Cornish Wreckers
Twelve Walks on the Lizard
Victorian Cornwall

Cover picture: the Cheesewring
Title page: Probus, on A390 just north of Roseland, has a magnificent
church tower and a charming little central square with this Victorian
lamp

This edition first published 1990 by
Tor Mark Press, Islington Wharf, Penryn, Cornwall TR10 8AT
Based on the earlier edition by W V Hunter; this edition
thoroughly revised by the publishers.
ISBN 0-85025-322-5
Printed in Great Britain by Swannack Brown & Co Ltd, Hull

*One of the commoner hazards
of the Cornish lanes*

Contents

Introduction

Knowing where to go to escape the season's crowds can make all the difference to your holiday in Cornwall and this guide tells you how. It is not a book about the obvious places to go such as St Ives, Polperro or Mevagissey, Land's End or the Lizard. It is a book about the quieter corners of the county, still not discovered by the average holiday-maker.

Cornwall is a place where a written guide is needed – unlike the Lake District say, where all is self-evident. The more you know, the more you can enjoy your holiday. Quiet by-roads in deep woodland, interesting old mining districts and secluded parts of the coast can still be found and exploration of them will add to your holiday enjoyment. In this book you will find suggestions both for the fit and active, including places with attractive coastal walks of a mile or two, and also parking places where those physically unable to leave their car can sit and enjoy a fine view.

It is a popular fallacy that Cornwall's roads are desperately overcrowded in season; in fact it is just the main through routes which get crowded, especially at weekends, and compared to many counties Cornwall has an unusual network of minor roads which make excellent alternatives to the A roads; these minor roads are a legacy of the days when mining was widespread and pack-horses trod a complex pattern of criss-cross routes between long-lost mines, quays and smelting houses.

Nearly all these roads have one common factor – the high 'hedges' which border them. These are not hedge-rows as in other counties but high banks of stone and earth from which springs undergrowth of one sort or another. The result is an all too effective barrier to the view the motorist might otherwise have. On open roads this is less noticeable but in the lanes the only view may be a glimpse from a field gate. As some compensation, these roadside banks are full of colourful flowers – primroses, foxgloves and a mass of bluebells, white garlic and pink campion to name but a few.

It is as well not to take the car too close to this lush growth: apparently harmless ferns and grass may conceal a projecting granite boulder. Constant attention by the driver is necessary,

Woodland east of Wadebridge

An uncommon hazard of the Cornish lanes

listening as well as watching, and you must be ready to reverse into a passing space if necessary.

One tour has been included, the last in the book, which does visit places which become congested in summer. We have included it because so many of the places are particularly worth visiting, but as a complete tour it is best undertaken outside the main holiday season. We make some suggestions how to modify it when the traffic is likely to be heavy.

To get the most from your holiday, the average road atlas is not really adequate. We strongly recommend the Ordnance Survey Landranger series (1:50,000): sheet 203 covers Land's End and the western half of the Lizard, sheet 200 Newquay and Bodmin, sheet 204 Truro and Falmouth, sheet 201 Plymouth and Launceston and sheet 190 the north coast.

If you are considering joining the National Trust, we also recommend you do so right at the beginning of your holiday. Because the Trust owns and preserves much of the finest coastal scenery, you might almost save the cost of membership by the free parking members receive at NT car parks! There are also many fine houses and gardens owned by the Trust in Cornwall.

The main through routes

The main roads of Cornwall have been immensely improved in the last twenty years, with by-passes opened along which traffic flows smoothly even in high summer, but there are still major bottlenecks which should be avoided if at all possible over the weekend period, as some visitors leave and others arrive. The places bypassed are often worth a diversion to visit now that they are quieter than they were.

The main trunk road is the A30, which enters Cornwall at Launceston and bypasses the town. The old road, now A388, winds across the Tamar at Polston Bridge into Launceston, which is an attractive town with a Norman castle and a church with excellent exterior carving – particularly surprising since the stone is hard granite. At Five Lanes, eight miles west, it is worth diverting into the extremely picturesque village of Altarnun for another fine church, St Nonna (mother of St David), which has remarkable carved bench ends. Altarnun is Cornwall's largest parish and the church is known as 'the cathedral of the Moor'.

From this point the road turns south-west across the wilds of Bodmin Moor, which is a granite mass not unlike Dartmoor but on a smaller scale. The scenery of open moorland crowned by granite tors is unlike that of any other main road in Cornwall; mists are frequent and this is one of the few parts of the south-west peninsula where snow falls most years – though it seldom lasts long and the County Council must employ more snow ploughs per inch of snow than any other in Britain!

From the celebrated Jamaica Inn one can see the highest point in Cornwall, Brown Willy, to the right of the road. Two miles further on, the original route of the turnpike road (first established in 1769) went through the hamlet of Temple; travelling south, it is still possible to follow the original road, which gives a true feeling of the high moor and is well worth an extra five minutes on the journey.

The A30 now bypasses Bodmin, still the county town although most county town functions are these days exercised at Truro, including the assizes. From the bypass you can see to the east tantalising views of the deep and wooded valleys of the river Fowey and its tributaries. From the roundabout at Lanivet, where the A391 diverges, the road is fast across Goss Moor to Indian Queens, but not a dual carriageway so it is

7

Altarnum, a picturesque village just off the A30 with a magnificent parish church dedicated to St Nonna

notoriously dangerous. The skyline to the south is dominated by the spoil-heaps of the china-clay workings, which are visible from many parts of the county. Occasionally, when seen in the distance with the sun shining on them, they look like distant Alps, but they are not at their best from Goss Moor.

Once past the bottleneck of Indian Queens one leaves behind the moorland and the clay tips and enters a green rolling countryside of small farms; the road gives surprisingly extensive views towards both coasts, but in summer the driver will be preoccupied with the slow moving traffic until the Redruth bypass is reached. Redruth, Pool and Camborne are effectively a single long town at the centre of what was once a major mining area and which still has a working tin mine, South Crofty. There are also preserved steam engines at Pool, in the care of the National Trust, and these are well worth visiting; but apart from its industrial archaeology (see the 'excursion' later in this book) and the view from the top of Carn Brea, the area has little to attract the holiday-maker. The port of Hayle and Penzance itself are also bypassed, but most visitors will want to explore Penzance.

As you approach it, the traffic can still grind to a total halt. Once you reach Penzance station, it is best to follow the harbour road because the town centre is narrow and crowded. Car parking is possible on the Esplanade beyond the harbour, and the pedestrian routes up into the town are pleasant – there is a surprising early Victorian area. Driving westward, you can delay turning inland again to rejoin the A30 beyond where the sign suggests you should, and carry on into the fishing port of Newlyn before turning right, but this can be very congested in season.

From Penzance westward the A30 is narrow, sinuous and entirely suitable for horse-drawn traffic – a reminder of what most of the main roads of Cornwall were like not that long ago. Past Sennen, you finally arrive thankfully at the Land's End.

The main alternative route into Cornwall, coming from Exeter, is to take the fast A38, bypass Plymouth, cross the suspension bridge at Saltash (toll when leaving Cornwall, free when entering) and take the A38 to Liskeard and then the A390 through St Austell to Truro. Generally this is a slower road than the A30. Before 1961 when the bridge was opened, all traffic went by the Torpoint ferry, which can still be thoroughly recommended for the stirring views it gives of the Hamoaze (part of Plymouth Sound) with its Royal Naval dockyards and shipping.

Whether going via Torpoint and the A374, or by the A38, it is worth making a diversion to St Germans for the fine church which once served Cornwall as a cathedral, and preserves one of the most striking Norman doorways in Britain.

Liskeard, now bypassed, is an attractive hill-town which was one of Cornwall's four Stannary towns, from which Cornish miners once had effective self-rule and where all tin was stamped to show tax had been paid on it.

The A38 continues west from here down the Fowey valley, through dense woods with the trout-filled river burbling (or in winter roaring) close beside the road. These are some of the finest woodlands in the county and extend up the various tributaries to the north. The villages between the Fowey and the southern edge of Bodmin Moor, for example Warleggan, St Neot and Cardinham, are well worth exploring.

The main route west is however the A390, through Lostwithiel, the Norman capital of Cornwall and another

This dramatic view of Brunel's bridge over the Tamar is taken from the Plymouth side, where a car park allows you to take a short rest and at the same time pay homage to the great engineer.

Stannary town, the straggling St Blazey and then St Austell. At the roundabout at the east end of St Austell, it is worth turning left for a mile down to the early Victorian port of Charlestown, beloved of film-makers producing costume drama, where there is a shipwreck museum. Two miles north of St Austell on the A391 is the Wheal Martyn china clay museum.

Before reaching Truro the A390 passes through Grampound, which was a bustling port called Ponsmur in Norman times; when the river silted up, a bridge was built over the Fal and the place became known as 'Grand pont'. Much later, Grampound became a famous 'rotten borough'. Next comes Probus, where the church has a most elegant tower, and then Tresillian, pleasantly situated at the head of a creek. Truro itself is a most attractive city and deserves to be explored on foot in a leisurely manner.

The A390 then heads towards St Agnes, and it is possible to join the A30 if you are going further west. Alternatively, there is a continuation of the more southerly route towards Penzance, by way of the A39 and A394. For much of the way, this is a narrow and winding route; between Truro and Carnon Downs in particular it carries dense traffic in season and on the long climbs heavy vehicles cause considerable queues. As with many other roads in Cornwall, it is a pleasure to use when quiet, but not when traffic has reached a certain density.

The stretch from Devoran to Perranarworthal is of particular interest: Devoran on Restronguet Creek was once a port, when it was at the lower end of a railway which served the mining areas between here and Redruth and Chacewater. The railway lasted from 1824 to 1915. From Devoran a branch of the Creek flows alongside the road; the tide flows right up to the Norway Inn and the old foundry buildings at Perranwharf (being developed as a Heritage Centre) where ships once delivered timber and loaded mine machinery. At high water of spring tides, this whole valley is a sheet of water, changing its appearance completely. The Norway Inn itself takes its name from the Norwegian timber ships which traded here in the nineteenth century, bringing Scandinavian timber for use in the mines.

The A39 descends to Penryn, a medieval town; and to Falmouth, a seventeenth century town which rapidly displaced Penryn as a port. The A394 avoids both, and also bypasses Helston and Marazion, both of which merit exploration, although Marazion becomes overcrowded in season. (The main car parks are on the Penzance side of the village, so go round the bypass and then turn back along the coast.) The A394 then rejoins the A30 just short of Penzance.

In the other direction, it is possible to use the A39 from near Tresillian (east of Truro) to travel northwards through Indian Queens, St Columb, Wadebridge (with a fine old bridge over the Camel) and Camelford to near Bude, but this is a very slow road if you have any distance up-country to travel when you leave Cornwall. Wadebridge in particular is in desperate need of a bypass.

Off the beaten track

During the holiday season certain beaches and roads in Cornwall become overcrowded whilst others do not. Local knowledge such as this is not easily acquired by visitors, even those who enjoy poring over maps. On the whole, eastern Cornwall is less crowded than the west, except on the through routes and in the main resorts, but even in the west there are quieter places.

The Eastern Shore of Mounts Bay

Loe Bar, though close to the busy tourist harbour of Porthleven, is remarkably unspoilt and with a little effort you can find privacy and near-solitude on this shingle beach even on a busy day. It can be reached easily by taking the B3304 Porthleven Road out of Helston. After a mile or so, at the top of Penrose Hill, Loe Bar is signed.

There are National Trust car parks here with sea views, and a walk of about half a mile to Loe Bar. This is a truly off-the-beaten-track stretch of coast which offers very pleasant picnic places on the low grassy cliffs overlooking the Bay, with the long expanse of Loe Bar immediately below. The beach itself is highly dangerous; it shelves steeply just below water level, causing a dangerous undertow, so on no account bathe there and keep young children away from the water's edge. There have been many deaths here, because the beach is deceptively attractive.

At the far end of Loe Bar is a memorial to the men lost with the frigate *HMS Anson* in 1807, another victim of the deceptive beach. The ship was in trouble and the captain tried to beach her not realising that the beach shelves so abruptly that it is like an underwater cliff of shingle. Although many escaped because a mast fell towards the land, over fifty seamen died just a few yards from the shore. Among the helpless spectators was Henry Trengrouse, a cabinet-maker, who later developed a life-saving apparatus which fired a line from a musket. He spent a great deal of time, effort and his own money; this simple idea was later responsible for saving thousands of lives throughout the world but, as is often the case with inventors, Trengrouse was unrecognised in his own time and died in penury.

The Bar is a treasure house for pebble hunting, with a variety of beautiful and unusual pebbles hard to equal anywhere in Britain. There are extensive walks across the shingle of the Bar and on to Gunwalloe, or inland towards Helston through the woods of Penrose alongside the Pool. Loe Pool is a noted haunt of water fowl, particularly of sea duck in winter. Note the tamarisk bushes which grow here despite the exposed position, and the areas of wild mesambryanthemum which cascade down the cliffs.

The observant will notice that there appears to be no outlet from the Pool to the sea, even though it is fed by a river and several streams. The shingle bar has impounded it completely and in former times a way had to be cut through the bar to release the trapped waters in time of flood. Now, however, a tunnel cuts through the bar so that the water flows out from the low cliff across the beach.

Loe Bar can also be reached more circuitously by turning right off the Helston–Lizard Road A3083 by the entrance to Culdrose Naval Establishment, about two miles out of Helston. This turning leads to Carminowe and then up to Chyvarloe. At the three-way junction, take the Loe Bar Sands lane, which leads to a small National Trust car park. Again you will have to walk the last half mile if you go this way and this car park has no view, but on a clear day there is a marvellous view from the low cliffs northward past Porthleven to Trewavas Head, with the expanse of the Pool in the foreground. Only the length of the Bar – about half a mile – separates the end of the footpath here from the footpath mentioned earlier, coming from Porthleven.

Another quiet corner of Mount's Bay just south of here is Winnianton. Go back to the three-way junction and take the lane down to Gunwalloe. By Berepper Post Office and opposite the inn a short lane leads down to Gunwalloe Fishing Cove and the cliffs; this is best explored on foot. The next settlement clusters round the Hazelphron Inn, near the cliffs of the same name, and the road then climbs over and round a small headland, to drop down to the expanse of grass and sand at Winnianton. Here, in Church Cove, is the little fifteenth century church of Winnianton, huddled in the lee of its own small headland, with the unusual feature of a separate bell-tower. There is ample parking at the farm, good bathing in either of the coves, a café conveniently sited but unobtrusive from the beaches, and clifftop walks for the energetic. The more northerly cove, Jangye-ryn, is also known as Dollar Cove from the wreck of a Spanish galleon bearing bullion; gold coins have been found here and various attempts made to locate the source of the treasure, without success.

Southward over the next outcrop of rocks is Poldhu Cove, where a monument on the headland to the south commemorates the first wireless signal from Europe to America sent from here in 1901. Poldhu can only be reached from Winnianton on foot. By car you have to go back to Culdrose, follow the Lizard road for three miles, then turn right towards Mullion.

Godrevy Point

A similar locality on the North coast, offering ample clifftop parking space with a beach below, is at Godrevy near Gwithian, at the north-east end of St Ives Bay. It is approached by the B3301 either from Portreath or from the south; leave the A30 at the roundabout a mile east of Hayle, taking the road towards Hayle but then almost immediately turning right on B3301. The road follows the inland edge of a very extensive area of towans (sand-dunes) formed by sand blown from St Ives Bay, to the pleasant little village of Gwithian. The B3301 continues north from Gwithian to a sharp bend by the narrow bridge carrying the road over the old Red River – which was until recently well named, as a result of tin-mining pollution in its upper reaches near Camborne. Turn sharp left here on an unclassified road which goes seaward, signposted Godrevy Point. Round the corner of the little headland this opens out onto the expanse of Godrevy Towans where there is extensive car-parking on land now in the care of the National Trust. This is the point where the shoreline begins to rise again to form the line of high cliffs eastward towards Portreath, after the low coast and dunes of St Ives Bay and the inlet of the Hayle River. Offshore on Godrevy Island is the unmanned lighthouse and there is a sweeping view across to Carbis Bay and St Ives.

This is a good place for bathing, for dabbling in the rock pools or for collecting shells and pebbles at low water. For the energetic, there is a three mile walk along the broad expanse of firm yellow sands exposed here as the tide recedes, right to the mouth of the Hayle estuary. In the other direction, there is a fine walk of similar length along the clifftop path round Godrevy Point and Navax Head to Hell's Mouth, and back along the road. This part of the shore has been noted for seals, although their numbers have been reduced by pollution. They may be seen on the inaccessible shore below the cliffs or by the rocks a short way out from the tide's edge. At Hell's Mouth the cliffs rise sheer from the sea to about 250 feet and great care

Godrevy Point, inspiration for Virginia Woolf's novel To the Lighthouse

should be taken, particularly with children. There have been several cliff tragedies here, some by accident and some by design. There are views towards St Agnes Head about eight miles away, where the little rounded eminence of St Agnes Beacon shows clearly.

A path continues along the cliff edge all the way to Portreath – one of the best sections of the coastal path, which began life as the route taken along the cliff on foot or on horseback by the 'coast watchers' – the coastguard men looking for wrecks and the preventive men looking for smugglers. The B3301 continues from Godrevy past Hell's Mouth and along the clifftops, on what are called Reskajeage Downs, but from a car there is not much of a view because the cliff edge is a field away; however there are numerous stopping places en route.

Chapel Porth

A little further along the north coast, the small cove south of St Agnes known as Chapel Porth is worth visiting. It is

View from the cliffs at Chapel Porth, looking towards St Agnes; a century ago, mining was still the mainstay of the economy and tourism was almost unknown

approached from the B3277 Truro to St Agnes road, turning left just after the St Agnes Model Village. Chapel Porth is another area preserved by the National Trust and thus relatively unspoiled. The car park near the beach tends to be full in season, but there is another nearer the top of the hill. Because of the rip-currents here the beach is controlled by lifeguards and the permitted bathing area can become very crowded in season.

The cliff walks in both directions are very rewarding, with numerous reminders that this was a mining area before it became a holiday destination. To the north are the forbidding old engine houses of Wheal Coates, halfway up the cliff below St Agnes Beacon, and in and around St Agnes itself are many old engine houses. The beach at Trevaunance Cove was once an active harbour, overlooked by West Kitty Mine.

The next valley on the road out of St Agnes towards Perranporth is Trevallas Coombe. In the dip down at Barkla Shop, a footpath leads inland towards Wheal Butson and the remains of a viaduct which carried the Newquay to Chacewater branch line. To the left another footpath leads down Jericho Valley, beautiful in early summer, to Trevallas

Porth. The lower part of the valley shows more of the extensive workings of Blue Hills Mine, which dominated the landscape a hundred years ago. The remains of a small 'stamps', for crushing tin ore, can still be seen as well as the water wheel which powered it. For further information on the mining industry, readers might like to refer to *Cornish Mining – at the Surface* and *Underground*, both in this series.

This valley can also be reached by car by going to the top of the hill out of Barkla Shop and taking the lane to Cross Coombe by the school. This is a narrow, twisting, surfaced track with few passing places but adequate parking at the bottom. From here the small rocky cove can be explored as well as the valley inland.

North of Newquay

Further north, beyond Newquay, there is an interesting diversion from the B3276 coast road to Trevose Head, but is can only be recommended out of season because of the camping and caravanning sites which clog the narrow roads.

Trevose Head is the principal headland between Land's End and beyond Bude – in fact to Hartland Point where the Bristol Channel begins. An important lighthouse has been sited here since 1840. Walk out onto the separate headland known as Dinas Head and the lighthouse can be seen across Stinking Cove. On the cliffs to the south is a feature similar to the better known Devil's Frying Pan near Cadgwith on the Lizard; there is a massive funnel-like opening where the roof of a huge sea cave has collapsed.

Another headland worth exploring is Pentire Point and the Rumps at the north or Polzeath side of the Camel estuary. Like many of the best scenic stretches of cliffs along the coast, these are owned by the National Trust, thereby safeguarding what is probably the finest heritage of Cornwall. To reach Pentire Point, take the B3314 out of Wadebridge – a left turn at the top of the hill. Follow the road for about four miles, then take the Polzeath signs. Within a mile, fork right signed New Polzeath then take a further right to Pentire Point, clearly marked by a National Trust sign. There is good parking in the yard of Pentire farm.

A path starts from the track a little way back, leading down to Pentireglaze Haven, a deep incision in the rocky shore where ore from a local lead mine was once shipped. From the car park there are walks around Pentire Point (with a fine view of the

The headland known as The Rumps; even in the season you will meet only a few other walkers on the cliff paths here

mouth of the Camel, the Doom Bar sands and across to Stepper Point on the other shore) to the extension of the main headland called the Rumps, with more splendid views. The Rumps themselves are geologically remarkable, being made of volcanic lava thrown up in remote times by undersea eruptions. There was an Iron Age cliff castle on the extremity here, defended by a wide ditch and bank, both clearly traceable across the neck.

On the return journey you may like to call at Portquin further along the coast. This is often referred to as the village that died. What remains today is in the care of the National Trust. In the nineteenth century it was a thriving fishing and mining village, but the nearby antimony mine at Doyden failed and many of the miners emigrated to Canada. An even greater tragedy occurred later in the century, when most of the remaining able-bodied men and boys were lost in a fishing disaster.

A pleasant stroll can be taken on Stepper Point, the twin headland to Pentire on the other side of the Camel. From

Portquin – the village that died

Padstow, turn right off the Newquay Road B3276 on leaving the port and proceed through the hamlet of Crugmeer to Hawker's Cove, where there is a car park by an attractive beach (Harbour Cove); a path leads on past the old quarry to Stepper Point itself.

West of Fowey

A corner of the south coast that is well off the beaten track and is ideal for a quiet half day excursion is Gribbin Head, the promontory to the west of Fowey, though you will need to leave your car to explore it fully. It is marked by a tall square tower which was erected in 1832 as a day mark for mariners, guiding them towards the Fowey river entrance which was otherwise difficult to discern from the sea.

Take the A3082 off A390 a mile or so east of St Austell; follow the road round the Par one-way system and as you climb up a steep hill out of Par take a right turn to Polkerris and Menabilly Beach. This runs along the peninsula with views across St Austell bay to the right. Pass the turning to Polkerris and continue to the car park on the right as the lane ends. This is close to the entrance of Menabilly, the ancestral home of the Rashleigh family and later of Daphne du Maurier, the novelist.

A clearly marked track leads past Menabilly Barton down to a small cove where you can either turn left towards Fowey or right along the coastal path to the tower. From the tower it is another two miles along the coastal path to Polkerris – a splendid cliff walk.

Polkerris can be reached by car by taking the turn to the left on the return journey. This one-time fishing cove has a small harbour, post office and pub and is well worth a visit. Access by car is virtually impossible and visitors are recommended to use the car park on the right as you descend into the village. From here it is a walk of a few hundred yards.

Trefusis Point

Near Falmouth a pleasant outing by car and foot is round Trefusis Point, between Flusing and Mylor Harbour or Churchtown as it is sometimes called. Mylor Harbour can be reached by taking a turning almost opposite the Norway Inn on the A39 at Perranarworthal, midway between Truro and Falmouth. Follow the signs to Mylor Bridge, then to Mylor Churchtown, where it is usually possible to park in the boatyard car park. This is a very large and active boating centre, with moorings extending right out into Carrick Roads. The famous fleet of Falmouth harbour oyster boats, which dredge the Fal, have their main headquarters here and can sometimes be seen racing as well as working.

A footpath leads south past the dinghy sailing club towards Trefusis Point and right round to the charming village of Flushing. There is an uninterrupted view across Carrick Roads and the anchored shipping to St Mawes and then, as one reaches the point, towards Falmouth harbour and town. Dutch engineers were responsible for changing the name of the old village from Nankersey to Flushing, when they came over to build Falmouth's quays. Later the ships' captains lived here, away from the rabble of common seamen who inhabited Falmouth. A pedestrian ferry plies back and forth.

The walk from Mylor Harbour to Flushing can also be done in the opposite direction, though parking is more difficult in Flushing. It is best to go through the village, follow the road to the left by the water's edge and park on the road to the beach. Continue along this road to start the walk to Trefusis.

King Harry Ferry is most people's favourite approach to Roseland

Excursions

Roseland

Any peninsula, accessible only from one direction, tends to remain relatively untouched and this is the secret of Cornwall as a whole, a tongue of land thrust out into the Atlantic with the spirit of 'a land apart'. But within Cornwall the Roseland peninsula, with St Mawes near its tip, has enjoyed the same kind of island seclusion on a lesser scale, and remains one of the least spoiled areas of the south-west.

Its landward limits cannot be precisely defined. Some people regard the whole area south of the A390 between the Tresillian River and St Austell as Roseland, but Roseland proper lies south-west of a line drawn from Ruanlanihorne on the Fal to Portloe on Veryan Bay. The tidal Fal is the northern boundary, separating Philleigh parish from Tregothnan, the wooded estate on the opposite shore owned by Lord Falmouth. To the west are Carrick Roads and to the east and south the open sea.

To reach Roseland, one can turn south off the A390 St Austell-Truro road along a variety of routes, mostly signposted to St Mawes, but the more romantic approach is via the King Harry Ferry. The venerable chain ferry runs a regular shuttle service to and fro in the summer months (out of season half hourly, on the hour and half-hour going east and on the quarters going west) and the overall time in queueing and crossing should not exceed 30 to 45 minutes. This ferry is actually a link on the B3289, which three miles further joins the A3078 to St Mawes. A short detour to the right from this junction takes one to St Just-in-Roseland church, celebrated for its creekside position and its wooded churchyard, with a profusion of semi-tropical shrubs; in fact it is more like a garden than a churchyard, and an extraordinarily peaceful spot. There was much storm damage in winter 1990, however.

St Mawes is an attractive large village which deserves to be explored on foot. If you are prepared for a short walk, take the turning signposted to the castle and leave the car there. From the car park there is a good view across to Falmouth; the passenger ferry across from St Mawes harbour can be a very pleasant trip. Alternatively, take the main road into St Mawes, where there is a car park nearer the harbour.

The Percuil River reaches Carrick Roads at St Mawes, and

divides the tip of the Roseland peninsula into two separate arms. In order to reach the other arm, it is best to take the A3078 back north for five miles to Trewithian, and then turn back southward on the more easterly arm. (There is a short cut, signposted Polhendra and Lanhay, but it is quite narrow.) Some two miles south of Trewithian, one reaches the pleasant little village of Gerrans, with its spired church. Here a road leads down to the nearby cove of Portscatho (or Portscatha: placename spellings in Roseland are undogmatic) where you should use the car park above the village as there is no parking further down. Continuing south from Gerrans the first road on the right leads to Percuil, a popular boating place about a mile upstream from St Mawes. There is a perfect picnic spot on this road to Percuil, on a grassy slope high above the winding river with a wide view inland to the north.

The main road leads south from Gerrans towards St Anthony Head, passing Trewince and Froe and seeming to get ever narrower between deep hedgebanks in true Cornish style. The sea is very close on the left, though not visible. At Porth Farm there is a National Trust car park, from which a walk of a hundred yards brings you to the pleasant Towan Beach. In another mile, take the left fork to St Anthony Head, the property of the National Trust, where there is a car park facing an extensive view westward to Falmouth and south beyond the Helford River. For anyone physically unable to leave their car, this car park offers one of the finest views in Cornwall.

There is a path to the headland and beyond, another leading down to the lighthouse, and a third giving access to a series of sandy coves below, towards Carricknath Point. These are ideal for a day in summer and are surprisingly sheltered from all except south-westerly winds. Beyond the Point is the magnificently situated old manor of Place, fronting its own quiet backwater of St Mawes harbour. Tucked behind Place Manor is St Anthony's Church – one of the first churches to be dedicated in Britain. Legend has it that Joseph of Arimathea took refuge in this bay with his nephew, the boy Jesus, when trading for tin, and that they sheltered here from the storm while they repaired their vessel. Certainly there was an ancient shrine here and possibly a Celtic monastery.

North-east of Trewithian lie Veryan, approached by a very narrow road, with its curious round thatched houses, reputedly built by a vicar to keep the devil (who lurked in corners) away from the vicar's daughters; and the archetypal little fishing village of Portloe where there is a car park at the eastern end as the road turns inland again. The pub here has a good garden, ideal for children.

West Penwith

One of the most scenic stretches of road in all the far south-west is the B3306 from St Ives to St Just. Following the line of cliffs which fringe the north side of the Land's End peninsula, the road curves round the contour lines of hill after hill, about 450 feet above the sea. The view changes with every mile and one refreshing change is the lack of modern houses to mar the timeless character of the landscape. It is, however, for the most part a narrow road, not designed for the traffic it now bears in summer, and the driver cannot let attention wander. In places the road jinks through the centre of a cluster of farm buildings between walls of enormous granite boulders, but these hazards are all part of the strong character of west Cornwall and any major road widening would be out of place. Much of the route is across open moorland so there are opportunities to stop off the road. Not more than twelve miles as the gull flies, although perhaps twice that with all the twists and turns, there is nevertheless sufficient to see and visit in this stretch that a whole day could be spent here.

Leaving St Ives, the road forks off from the Penzance road close by the site of the once famous St Ives Consols tin mine; as the road ascends the shoulder of Rosewall Hill, one can see buildings surviving from other old mines.

At Zennor, follow the old road down into the village. A track, not for cars, leads between the church and the Tinners Arms (and then turns left in the farmyard) to Zennor Head. The twelfth century church is small and charming, and famous for its carved mermaid; legend says that a beautiful woman in a long dress used to visit the church to hear the singing of the chorister Matthew Trewhella, and ultimately lured him to the sea. The Wayside Museum at Zennor shows what can be achieved by an enthusiast, with extensive displays devoted to Cornish folk history.

Two miles beyond, at Treen, there is a footpath leading down to the next major promontory, Gurnard's Head. This coast is one long succession of cove, headland, cove, with the shore itself almost always inaccessible. Terrible seas come battering in to the rocks at the foot of these cliffs during onshore gales and shipwrecks along this exposed stretch of

Lanyon Quoit – one of Cornwall's most famous antiquities

coast have been frequent in the past; photographs of many of these can be found in Richard and Bridget Larn's *Shipwrecks around Land's End* in this series.

Inland, in another mile or so, are the granite-strewn slopes of Carn Galver and Watch Croft. In spring these moors are ablaze with the purple of foxgloves which grow everywhere among the gorse, heather and bracken, but at the time of year when the foxgloves are in bloom, beware adders, locally very numerous, which emerge from their winter lairs to bask on the sun-warmed rocks but are still too sluggish to move away at a person's approach as they do later in the summer.

On the higher moorlands inland there are numerous antiquities, such as the Nine Maidens and other stone circles, various tumuli, standing stones and quoits (dolmens) such as those at Zennor, Mulfra and Lanyon. These uplands behind the coastal hills are deserted now, but in prehistoric times were perhaps more densely settled than other parts of Cornwall.

A mile or so past the hamlet of Morvah, the B3306 begins to change in character; rows of cottages and an occasional ruined engine house are seen, instead of a bare landscape. But before we reach the old mining district that these herald, there is a turning on the right that should not be missed, leading down to the lighthouse of Pendeen Watch. For anyone unable to leave their car, turn right past the perimeter wall of the lighthouse and you will find a parking place overlooking the sea. There is a commanding view from here back along the coast towards Gurnard's Head, or in the other direction past the buildings of the old Levant mine towards Botallack.

Back on the coast road, the mining villages of Pendeen, Trewellard, Carnyorth and Botallack merge into one long string of granite cottages that were once the homes of miners who found employment in the dozen or so mines which worked tin and copper along the cliffs here. Levant and Botallack were the two most famous, both working far out beneath the restless waters of the Atlantic. At Geevor Mine in Trewellard there is a mining museum; at the surface there is a museum with exhibits and an excellent video is shown. Tours are organised both of the surface and of the underground workings.

A little further on you come to the village of Botallack; at the entrance to the village bear right, then turn right (unmade road) and park just beyond the Counthouse; again there is a view from the car park. It is an easy descent from here to the two famous engine houses perched at the foot of the cliff.

After the steep little descent and ascent to negotiate the Tregaseal Valley, the road enters St Just, the principal 'church-town' of the area and the capital of this former mining district. It is neat and clean, with a spacious square where Wesley preached more than once to the miners – but where there remains a greater choice of pub than is generally found in Cornwall! One can turn inland here on the A3071 across to Penzance or continue westward on B3306 towards Sennen and Land's End. While here, don't miss a short trip down to Cape Cornwall and its neighbouring cliffs; it is possible to walk right round the Cape or to climb to the summit where the tiny mine stack stands. There are walks either way along the cliffs.

Carn Gloose, a rocky eminence about half a mile south of Cape Cornwall, can also be reached by road. In St Just, take the road to Cape Cornwall; turn left 300 yards after the school. Carn Gloose makes a superb picnic spot, with a magnificent view over the Cape, the Brisons offshore and Whitesand Bay to the south. Close at hand is Ballowal Carn, an intricate bronze age burial mound.

Another interesting road is the B3311 from St Ives to Penzance. This leaves the St Just road by St Ives Consols and then heads for the curious hamlet of Halsetown on the moors behind Knill's monument. This was a settlement artificially

Carn Gloose makes a splendid picnic spot, with fine views even for those unable to move far from their car

created in the nineteenth century as a means of obtaining extra votes at a parliamentary election at a time when only householders could vote and the ballot was public not secret. By creating a new village, with all its tenants dependent on him, the owner of Halsetown helped assure his seat at Westminster.

The next hill ahead is Trink, with a fine view despite its quite modest elevation. To the left is its twin hill of Trencrom, with a picturesque summit strewn with gigantic granite boulders and outcrops. This was another mining area a century and more ago, and the old mining hamlet of Cripplesease back on the B3311 has an interesting surviving engine house. At the top of the climb from Nancledra there is a wide view over the neck of land connecting the Land's End peninsula with the rest of Britain, with St Michael's Mount at its southern end, and eastward to Godolphin Hill, Carn Brea and the heights of Carnmellis in the direction of Falmouth. About a mile further on, a lane leads off on the right up to Chysauster, the well-known Iron Age village which is certainly worth visiting, as it is well enough preserved to make it possible to imagine life here 2000 years ago. There are numerous lanes, tracks and paths onto the uplands, which are notable for their number and variety of prehistoric remains.

From Badger's Cross, where the Chysauster road turns off, the B3311 winds down towards the shore of Mount's Bay through the twists and turns of Gulval on the eastern outskirts of Penzance, so avoiding the traffic in the town centre.

Bodmin Moor

The moor's scenery is unlike that anywhere else in Cornwall; its character is comparable to Dartmoor further east, and much is accessible only on foot or horseback. The A30 bisects it (see page 7) but although there is a side road south from near Jamaica Inn to St Cleer, there are few other roads across the higher moor. Around the edges of the moor, however, there is a network of by-roads to be explored, giving access to some of the finest inland scenery in the county – roads which are quiet even in high summer, as they need to be because they are mostly very narrow indeed.

This excursion of about 70 miles is a circuit of the moor, and you can begin it wherever convenient to you, but we shall start at Bodmin. You will need a good map, preferably the Ordnance Survey 1:50,000, and an alert map-reader!

Either take the lane north through Boconnion, or go north-east on the A30, then turn north. The first village not to be missed is Blisland, with its very un-Cornish green and a church with a most remarkably restored interior, including a delicately painted rood screen. The pub on the green can also be recommended! Next northward again, either by Wenfordbridge and Lank, or across Delford Bridge, an ancient clapper bridge, and then back westward into St Breward where the village claims to be the highest in the county; there is an interesting sundial on the church porch.

From St Breward a number of side roads, some unfenced, lead north towards Camelford. Follow A39 and on the edge of the town, as the road narrows uphill, a right turn (through Tregoodwell) leads south-east in a direct line towards Rough Tor, 1311 ft above sea level. The road ends by the stream which flows down to Stannon Marsh – an area somewhat spoilt by a china-clay works; from the car park (with an attractive view for anyone unable to leave the car) there is an easy walk of a mile or so to the summit. After rain this may need stout shoes in the low-lying places, but the view from the summit is rewarding on all sides and OS maps will enable you to identify the various tors.

Continuing the circuit of the moor, return past Rough Tor Farm and take the first right through Davidstow Woods. After two miles, you will find yourself on a disused airfield. Turn right, heading south-east across Davidstow Moor towards Bray Down (1138 ft and also worth the climb) and picturesque Altarnun. Then east for two miles on the A30, bear right at Plusha (B3257) and then turn right and thread your way south through Trevadlock, Trebartha, North Hill, Bathpool, Rillaton and Rilla Mill, which are strung out along the sparkling, trout-filled Lynher River. (If you have had enough of narrow lanes, you can follow B3257/B3254 from Plusha to Upton Cross.)

At Rilla Mill, turn back westwards through Upton Cross across the open moorland just north of Caradon Hill. Here there are some striking mining remains, the Hurlers stone circle, Long Tom cross and the Cheesewring. Continue south-west, passing the inscribed King Doniert's Stone and then

Rough Tor

Clapper bridge on Bodmin Moor

Golitha Falls on the River Fowey, to the right of the road. (St Neot is a short diversion away: the church has magnificent medieval stained glass.)

At Doublebois this road joins the A38 westward, following the Fowey as it gathers strength rapidly from its tributaries. We leave the river near Bodmin Parkway station and return to Bodmin to complete the circuit of the Moor. The circuit is about 70 miles and will take anything from three hours to a whole day.

An excursion round Cornwall's industrial past

Most visitors to Cornwall come for the scenery, the climate and the people, but it is impossible not to notice the numerous relics of the industrial past, especially the mining industry. This brief excursion has been designed to take the visitor who is inquisitive about this past round the major sites in one small area, south of Redruth. Please be warned, it is not designed as a scenic route – mining was a major polluter as well as the mainstay of the economy – and not everyone is able to savour the romance of past industry. You will however see some things that make Cornwall unique: nowhere else was tin mined from lodes with the same intensity as here.

Start at the Norway Inn, on the A39 at Perranarworthal, halfway between Truro and Falmouth. Norwegian timber was once unloaded here for transport to the mines, until the creek silted up. Start towards Truro, and in under a mile, just after a garage, turn left (signposted Bissoe). To your left is the Carnon River, where until recently tin-streaming was carried on – the most ancient way of winning tin, by washing sand and gravel.

Forward at the crossroads (SP Mount Wellington Mine). Stop after the railway viaduct and look back at it: the stumps of piers are the remains of Brunel's original viaduct, one of 42 between Plymouth and Falmouth which for reasons of cost had to be constructed of wood. From each pier three graceful fans of timbers radiated out to support the massive beams on which the railway ran. On this section of line, they were not replaced until the 1920s.

Enter Bissoe, passing on the left the square chimney of an arsenic works. Arsenic is a by-product of tin-mining; its use as an industrial chemical and in herbicides and pesticides increased in the late nineteenth century and old spoil-heaps were reworked to extract it. Much of the sand in the Carnon valley remains poisoned by arsenic. Ahead of us is the Mount Wellington Mine, which closed in 1985 but is connected underground with Wheal Jane, and was worked after 1985 from there. Wheal Jane is one mile north-east, not working at the time of writing, but held in readiness for a possible rise in world tin prices. Cornish mining has for a century and more been a very precarious business enterprise.

Cross the bridge and turn right opposite the garage; carry straight on for 0.6 miles. Immediately below Mount Wellington's headgear, there is a parking place on the right; walk a few yards down a track to the right and you will see a red stream emerging beneath the embankment of the disused railway. This stream is the County Adit: an 'adit' is an underground drain from a metal mine, into which water from 'above adit' drained naturally and up to which water from 'below adit' could be pumped. Most mines had their own adit, but the Great County Adit was a cooperative venture, begun in 1748, which drained fifty or more copper and tin mines in the Gwennap, Redruth and Chacewater areas. In all there were some forty miles of tunnels.

The disused railway was the Redruth & Chasewater (sic), Cornwall's first true railway (as opposed to tramway) which opened in 1825 using horses till 1854, then locomotives to draw the wagons. It carried ore down the valley to Point, beyond Devoran, and most of its route can still be traced.

The village of Twelveheads lies directly ahead; its name comes from a sixteenth century stamping engine, driven by a water wheel, which had twelve stamp-heads to break up the ore.

However, rather than going into Twelveheads, retrace your steps and take the first right, which passes Mount Wellington; follow signs towards Carharrack. You will pass through the old United Mines area. One stamp engine house on the left is almost all that remains to be seen of what was one of the most extensive copper mines in the county, with over 80 miles of underground workings; twenty steam engines were at work in this locality. But the mines have left a despoiled landscape; 'reclamation' in this area for years involved dumping of household and other rubbish but perhaps in due course the land will be properly reclaimed.

At the junction keep right and in three quarters of a mile go left into St Day, which lies the other side of the B3298. This was once the capital of the copper-mining district and the church – built in 1828 and now in ruins – was designed to seat 2000. Nowadays St Day is not unattractive, but there is a curious uncertainty about it – neither town nor village.

In St Day, turn left, passing the church, then first left and left again along B3298; in approximately 600 yards, turn right (SP Chacewater) and in approximately half a mile turn left (SP Wheal Bush, Wheal Busy). The two neighbouring engine houses on the left are Wheal Unity Wood. Ahead on your left is a particularly striking stack, that of Killifreth mine. Cross the main road and in half a mile you will reach Great Wheal Busy on the right. This is an old mine, worked from the seventeenth century until the 1920s, though not continuously. Notice the lintels inscribed GREAT WHEAL 1872 BUSY MINE.

Retrace your steps to the crossroads and turn right; 300 yards on the left there is access to an engine house of the Killifreth Mine, which has been restored and made safe. Now follow the direct line of the old road through Scorrier and into Redruth. Ahead you will see Carn Brea, with an obelisk ostentatiously commemorating a member of the Bassett family. Due to vagaries of road numbering, the road is

The remains of Brunel's wooden railway viaduct across the Carnon Valley stand beside its replacement

sometimes B3297, sometimes A3047, but it is always straight ahead. Redruth has a one way system, inadequately signposted: follow signs to the station; avoid going under the railway bridge, then head for Camborne.

Between Redruth and Camborne lies Pool where two fine engines have been preserved and are in the care of the National Trust. They are open to the public in the summer months. That on the main road is a whim or winding engine, and the other a massive pumping engine. Continue towards Pool, passing the most important mine in Cornwall in the twentieth century, South Crofty. In half a mile, at the bottom of a hill and opposite the Tuckingmill Hotel, turn left. In a few hundred yards you will see a railway arch ahead of you, to the left. Stop just before the arch, and look back at the scene, recently 'refurbished'. Here on the Red River (stained until the late 1980s by the ore) were the surface workings of the greatest of all the tin mines, Dolcoath; this scene a century ago can be seen in another book in this series, *Cornwall's Engine Houses;* photographs of Dolcoath in the 1890s appear in *Cornish Mining – Underground,* also in this series.

33

Once under the railway arch, keep left. Pass the Brea Inn and bear right past the ivy-clad ruins of Tincroft; then turn right rather than crossing the railway and immediately turn right again (SP Four Lanes). Up a long hill, then turn left at the Countryman pub into Carnkie. This whole area has been much affected by mining since Tudor times and many stacks and engine houses are still standing. Follow the main route through Carnkie, crossing the moors south of Redruth; turn left after about a mile (SP Redruth B3297) and at traffic lights turn right towards Falmouth.

The next section is a detour to see Gwennap Pit, a semi-natural amphitheatre made famous by John Wesley preaching there to 'innumerable multitudes [among] unparalleled and inexhaustible mine workings'. It is worth seeing but the lanes are very narrow, and you could follow A393 to Ponsanooth, picking up the tour again there.

Approximately 700 yards after the traffic lights, turn left into Sandy Lane and continue another 700 yards till you come to a turning on the right with a white gate (set back and rather hard to spot) with the name 'Navrone'. Turn right here; at a T junction keep left. In due course you come to a right turn signed Gwennap Pit, and the pit is immediately on the right. After your visit, carry on along this road, down a hill with overhanging trees, turn right onto the B3298.

When you reach the main A393 do not join it but turn sharp left into Gwennap; although Gwennap parish was the centre of so much mining activity, the village itself seems never to have been affected, and remains in a world apart. Rejoin A393 south (left) to Ponsanooth, a village that made great use of waterwheels on the Kennall River to run among other things a smelting house, a paper mill, a wool mill, two corn mills and a guttapercha factory. One of the waterwheels remains. Further upstream there was a gunpowder factory, supplying the mines with explosive for blasting.

At the end of the village a narrow left turn leads under a railway viaduct (more stumps); to the right is Cosawes Country Park, with mobile homes, once the site of another gunpowder works. Now you rejoin the A39 and at Perran Wharf in 600 yards will see on the right the Perran Foundry. This at one time employed 400 people, covered six acres and exported steam engines all over the world; they were loaded on flat-bottomed barges and transhipped further downriver. There are plans to set up a mining Heritage Centre here.

If by now you are not surfeited with industrial archaeology, you could go on past the Norway Inn and turn right to Devoran and Point to trace the course of the Redruth & Chasewater railway along Devoran Quay where the containers for ore awaiting shipment are still visible. There are also pleasant walks around the creek here and at Feock.

A tour north from Newquay

Northwards from Newquay there is a road following much of the coastline to Bude and beyond, a stretch of cliffs with a rugged grandeur that is not exceeded anywhere in Britain. The inlet of the Camel estuary approximately halfway along this stretch of coast means a long detour inland to the lowest bridge point at Wadebridge but both north and south of this the views from a car are superb.

Of all the routes suggested in this book, this one is most likely to be congested: Padstow, Tintagel and Boscastle in the season are best appreciated either early in the morning or late in the evening and Wadebridge is a major bottleneck especially at weekends. From Whitsun to the end of August, it is best to be through Wadebridge before 9.30am. At the end of the tour we have made some suggestions for modifications in the high season.

Leave Newquay on A392, which is the northward continuation of the main seafront road. Turn left at the roundabout, signed B3276 Padstow, down to Porth where the road winds in tight curves round the sandy inlet. Trevelgue Head then lies on the left-hand side. From the sheer, almost overhanging cliffs about fifty yards from the road there is a fine view northwards of Watergate Bay, noted for surfing. A view of it opens up from the road itself before we drop down to Watergate Beach. Keep left here up the hill, signed Padstow, following the coast on an unclassified road that rejoins B3276 a mile or so further on at Trevarrian.

Another steep drop down to shore level comes at Mawgan Porth – one of the last haunts of mermaids in Cornwall, it is said! There is a narrow bridge over the stream here, then up again to the cliff tops beyond, about 300 feet above sea level. In winter, when the westerly gales blow, this is a very exposed spot, quite different from the summer months. Note how few flowers or shrubs grow in the gardens along this exposed coast, for they cannot live in the salt-laden gales, save perhaps tamarisks which survive even in the farm hedgerows.

About a mile further on are the famous Bedruthan Steps, which legend has it were the stepping stones of the giant Bedruthan. One of the rocks is supposed to be similar in profile to Elizabeth I and is consequently known as the Queen Bess Rock; whether you can spot this resemblance or not, Bedruthan Steps are well worth exploring. The area is now in the hands of the National Trust, who have done much to reclaim and restore this famous beauty spot which was becoming badly eroded. The beach can only be explored at low water. Please take heed of the tide: in the past many people have been cut off here and, alas, a few drowned through their own foolishness. There is access to the beach only in summer, an excellent café, information centre and National Trust shop, with good car parking.

At the little sandy inlet of Porthcothan, about two miles further, B3276 leaves the coast and cuts directly across towards Padstow. Alternatively you can leave the main road and turn left opposite the Tredrea Inn as you climb out of Porthcothan, signed Treyarnon; although this route is very slow, being no more than a lane, it does allow you to explore Treyarnon, Constantine and Harlyn Bays, which because of the difficulty of access are often reasonably quiet. At low water there is plenty of sand. Nearby Trevose Head, with good walks, is described on page 17.

Padstow is a fascinating port with a long history as a haven of refuge on this exposed stretch of coast, although entering the Camel estuary in the days of sail was always exceedingly dangerous, giving rise to the evil reputation of the sandy Doom Bar across its entrance. There are some fine old buildings by the harbour as well as a walk seawards along the estuary that should not be missed. Padstow was once a railway terminus and the disused track of the single line up the estuary to Wadebridge is now a foot and cycle path. (Cycles can be hired in Wadebridge.)

Leave Padstow on A389 for Wadebridge (9 miles) through Little Petherick. A mile or so after St Issey there is a wide view to the left over the estuary, looking towards the open sea. Joining A39, our route drops into Wadebridge, over the handsome bridge over the Camel. This ancient bridge originally had 17 arches, but three of them have been blocked up. It is reputedly built on piles of wool. In half a mile, at the top of the hill out of the town, turn left off A39 onto B3314, signed Port Isaac. We get a glimpse of the Camel again by the

The beach at Polzeath – famous for surfing

narrow humpbacked bridge near Trewornan; the marshes here are a haunt of geese in the winter months. By-roads to the left lead to Rock, on the estuary opposite Padstow, and then to Trebetherick and Polzeath, with their sandy beaches close by the open sea. (See page 17 for Pentire Point with walks along the cliffs.) B3314 turns sharply right, following the line of the coast but more than a mile inland. With such striking scenery, it is a pity no road runs along these cliff tops as it does further west. Continue past St Endellion church to a left turn two miles further on for Port Isaac. This is B3267, which goes down into the narrow streets of this one-time fishing port. Park before you enter the old part, which was never intended for anything larger than a small cart: an extensive car park is provided on the right, off the road leading to Port Gaverne, with magnificent views northwards along the coast.

The road through Port Gaverne continues on to rejoin B3314. In another 5 miles we come to Delabole, an ugly straggling village. The vast slate quarry which has made Delabole famous can be seen a few hundred yards inland from the main road. Turn left in Rockhead, where Delabole's houses end, then first right to cut across country and join the road into

The Old Post Office at Tintagel – a fine example of a medieval Cornish manor house, looked after by the National Trust; Tintagel becomes very congested, and is best visited either early or late in the day

Tintagel. This is clearly marked. There is a steep hill down to the road junction, by some disused quarries, this whole area having been worked for slate for many centuries.

In two more miles B3263 enters Tintagel, legendary home of King Arthur. Off the main (Fore) Street there are various car parks, from which to walk to the Norman castle and much earlier monastic site on the cliffs. This is quite a climb on the way back, but the pilgrimage is worthwhile.

Back on B3263 the road follows the coast through Bossiney – a hamlet which once sent an MP to Westminster, no less a person than Francis Drake – then down and across the deep Rocky Valley to Boscastle. The winding harbour inlet here is second only to Tintagel as a tourist attraction; car parking space is provided alongside the stream running down to the sea.

Continue out of Boscastle on B3263, which leads to the A39 and a twelve mile run into Bude. If time permits, you can take the narrow road a mile out of Boscastle, clearly marked to Crackington Haven. This follows the coast; after only a short distance there is a National Trust sign 'High Cliff', the point where the cliffs reach their highest anywhere in Cornwall. Apart from scattered farms, this coastline is deserted. Crackington Haven is a mere hamlet nestling below Cambeak cliff. The road turns inland after Crackington, then drops back to the coast at Millook. From here it follows the cliff edge, with panoramic views above Widemouth, looking north of Bude towards Hartland Point in Devon. Lundy Island can be seen when the weather is clear. Beyond Widemouth, the cliffs become much lower and the coast road continues for another three miles before dropping down into Bude. This coastal route from Boscastle has much to recommend it, but it will inevitably be slow.

Bude is a very attractive holiday town; its isolation gives it its special charm and it has excellent beaches for swimming and surfing. Bude and its much older neighbour Stratton are both worth exploring, as are the remains of the old Bude Canal, built to transport sea sand inland.

The return leg of this tour can be made almost entirely down the A39 through Camelford and Wadebridge, by-passing St Columb, where the road back to Newquay is clearly marked. The journey north up the coast may have taken five hours, but coming back on the A39 should take just over one hour so if it is teatime when you reach Bude, don't despair! The only problem of course is Wadebridge, which you will find blocked most summer days until about 6pm; if you can delay your journey until after that, you should sail through quite happily.

An alternative we can recommend is to return down the A39 until just south of Camelford and then take B3266 down to Bodmin. Although a B road, this is surprisingly fast and straight. Join A389 and as you climb up into Bodmin there is a sign marked Redruth, up a steep hill by an old level crossing. Follow this to join the A30; at Indian Queens the Newquay road is clearly signposted.

This is a long tour, not less than five hours, and you may well wish to undertake parts of it rather than the whole; one suggestion is to divide it into two – Newquay to Padstow and Wadebridge to Bude – which would allow you to get through Wadebridge before the congestion builds up. If you are starting at lunch time, you might want to use the B3266 route to go northwards first, then make your way south along the coast from Bude or Boscastle, so passing through Wadebridge in the early evening.

Index